20 Ways to Cook
CHICKEN

Gail Duff

Thomas Harmsworth Publishing Company

First Published 1994 by
Thomas Harmsworth Publishing
Company
Old Rectory Offices
Stoke Abbott
Beaminster
Dorset DT8 3JT
United Kingdom

British Library Cataloguing-in-Publication
Data. A catalogue record for this book is
available from the British Library.

ISSN 1355-4050
ISBN 0 948807 19 9

Printed and bound in Great Britain by
BPC Paulton Books Ltd.

CONTENTS

INTRODUCTION

There can be few meats more versatile and economical than chicken. You can buy chicken every day of the week throughout the year and you could probably make a different dish with it on every one of those days.

Chicken can be roasted, poached, braised, casseroled, grilled, fried or stir-fried. It can be cooked on a stove or in an oven, chicken brick, pressure cooker or microwave oven, or over the coals of a barbecue. It can be made into hot meals or served as a salad and it also makes hearty, nourishing soups. You can buy whole chickens, fresh or frozen, plus portions, breasts, thighs, wings or drumsticks.

Nearly every country around the world has its own favourite chicken dish and every one is within your grasp. Change the herbs, the marinade, the cooking liquid or the spices. Serve your dish with rice, with pasta or potatoes and a variety of different vegetables. With chicken, you can go on a gastronomic tour.

It is excellent value for money and also, increasingly, is regarded as one of the healthiest meats. It has a relatively low fat content and a high percentage of its fat is unsaturated.

Ready-flavoured products are now available but are, however, never as good as those that you have prepared yourself from fresh, natural ingredients.

This book will tell you everything you need to know about preparing whole chickens and chicken pieces.

TYPES OF CHICKEN AVAILABLE

Whole chickens come fresh or frozen. Frozen birds tend to be cheaper and are likely to be indoor reared. Fresh birds can be either indoor or outdoor reared and are generally thought to have a better flavour. Free-range birds are usually the most expensive and are preferred for their fine flavour and for humanitarian reasons. Corn-fed chickens have a yellow skin and an excellent flavour due to a rich diet of maize. They are usually reared confined in sheds and runs.

Chicken portions may be more economical to buy if serving only one or two people, but be careful which you buy.

Chicken quarters are produced by simply slicing the chicken (usually a battery one) into four pieces. Effective, but difficult to eat and visually unattractive. For soup or stock they are fine, but if you intend to prepare a dinner party buy a whole chicken and joint it (see below). If the meal is for two, you can freeze the spare joints for another time.

Breast of chicken (boneless) can be bought if you need only lean meat. This is dense meat and the most expensive portion of the chicken, but a little will go a long way. It is good for stir-frying

 2

where small amounts of meat are mixed with vegetables. Whole chicken breasts can also be roasted (page 6).

*Chicken drumstick*s make economical family meals — fried, roasted, grilled or mixed into dishes such as paella. For more meat, choose chicken thighs and use them in a similar way to drumsticks.

PORTION SIZES

Whole chicken: One 3 - 3½ lb (1.4 - 1.6kg) chicken will serve four people.
Chicken portions: one per person
Boneless breast: 4 - 6 oz (125 - 175g) per person
Drumsticks: 3 per person
Thighs: 2 per person

STORING CHICKEN

Frozen chicken. If you intend to keep it, put it into your freezer as soon as you get it home. Store it for up to 3 months. If it is for eating within a few days, put the chicken in its wrapping onto a dish or a plate with high sides in the refrigerator. It will thaw within 12 hours but may be kept for up to three days in the refrigerator. Make sure that it is properly defrosted before cooking.

Fresh chicken will keep in the refrigerator for up to 48 hours. If you want to freeze one, keep it in its wrapper and freeze it in the coldest part of your freezer. Store it at normal freezer temperature for up to 3 months.

Chicken Portions. Put frozen portions into your freezer as soon as you get them home. Store them for up to 3 months. Defrost in the refrigerator for 6 to 8 hours. Some chicken joints, such

as drumsticks and thighs, come in large packs and you may wish to split these up for freezing. To freeze, lay them separately on a tray and put them into the coldest part of the freezer. When they are frozen, pack them into a polythene bag and seal them. Keep them in the freezer for up to 3 months. Defrost them in the refrigerator for 6 - 8 hours.

BASIC PREPARATION

Preparing a whole chicken for cooking is very simple. First, if it has been frozen, make sure that it is completely defrosted.

Feel just inside the body cavity. There are sometimes two pieces of clean, dry fat here. If they are still in place, pull them away and discard them.

If the ends of the feet are still on the chicken legs, these can be cut off, if wished, by taking a sharp meat knife and cutting through the joints. You will be cutting cartilage, not bone, and they should come off easily. Similarly, the ends of the wings can be cut away. Neither of these are edible and the chicken looks better when cooked if they are removed beforehand.

Season the inside of the body cavity and put in a bunch of fresh herbs or sprinkle in about 1 tablespoon dried herbs. Several slices of lemon inside the cavity will reduce fattiness and lighten the flavour. Where a recipe specifies the type of herb, use that. If the chicken is to have a stuffing, omit the herbs and lemon. The flavouring will come from the stuffing.

To truss the chicken, use fine cotton string. Tie the string to one leg, leaving one length long-

er than the other. Pass the long end around the parson's nose twice, then round the second leg twice and finally tie it securely to the shorter end.

Fresh chickens from independent butchers are often ready trussed. In order to prepare the chicken as described, you will need to remove the butcher's trussing string first.

Jointing a chicken into four pieces. Cut off the pieces of feet and the tips of the wings, as above.

Place the chicken on a work surface with the breast facing away from you. Hold one leg and, using a sharp meat knife, cut through the skin which separates the leg from the breast. Bend the leg gently outwards so the thigh bone comes away from the small oval hip bone, (called the oyster bone). Cut through the connecting tissue around the joint and take the leg away. Repeat with the other leg.

With one hand, push down on the skin on either side of the breast bone so that the line of the bone is clearly definable through the skin. Put the point of your knife to one side of the bone and cut downwards, with the knife following the bone. Separate the breast from the rib cage by making small strokes with the knife close to the bone. Cut around the wishbone and separate the top of the wing from the carcass in the same way as you did the leg. This will give you one piece comprising half the complete breast plus the wing attached. Remove the other half of the breast in the same way.

This will give you four large joints.

To joint the chicken into eight pieces, follow the instructions above to make four. Then cut the legs into two pieces at the joints giving you a drumstick and a thigh portion from each leg. Cut diagonally through the breast pieces about three quarters of the way along, giving you one large piece of breast and one wing with a piece of breast attached.

BASIC COOKING METHODS

Roasting a chicken. Heat the oven to 400F/ 200C/gas 6. Prepare and truss the chicken as above. Put the chicken into a roasting tin either on the base or on a rack. Season the outside of the skin. If wished, you can spread the skin with a little softened butter or baste it with oil. Sprigs of fresh herbs can be laid over the breast and legs. Cover the chicken with foil. Put it into the oven for 1 hour. Take away the foil. Continue cooking for 30 minutes or until the chicken skin is brown and crisp.

To test if it is cooked enough, push a fine skewer into the thickest part of the leg near where it joins the body. If the juices run clear, the chicken is cooked. If the juices are slightly pink, cook for a little longer.

Poaching a chicken. Poached chicken meat is very moist and can be carved like a roast chicken, diced and mixed into a sauce, or made into a salad. When poaching, use similar herbs and spices as are going into the final dish. So, if you are serving the chicken hot in a parsley sauce, put a large sprig of parsley inside it, or if cold in a curry-flavoured mayonnaise, rub either curry powder or curry spices such as cumin and coriander into the skin. Lemon slices lighten the flavour of poached chicken.

Put the prepared chicken into a saucepan and

pour in water to just cover the tops of the legs. Put in one small onion, halved, plus one carrot and one celery stick, both roughly chopped. Add a bunch of herbs that will complement the final dish plus a bayleaf. Bring the chicken to the boil on a medium heat. Cover, and simmer for 50 minutes, or until the chicken is tender.

Lift out the chicken. If you are serving it hot, let it stand for 10 minutes before jointing or dicing. If it is to be a cold meal, cool it completely at room temperature before dicing.

Pot roasting a chicken. Heat the oven to 350F / 180C / gas 4. Prepare the chicken as for roasting. Melt 1 oz (25g) butter in a large, flameproof casserole on a medium heat. Put in the chicken and brown it all over. Surround the chicken with a selection of prepared vegetables (carrots, celery, swede, celeriac, leeks, sliced onion) and pour in ½ pint (275ml) liquid (stock, wine, cider or a mixture). Bring the liquid to the boil. Cover the pan and put it into the oven for 1 hour 30 minutes. Check at 30 minute intervals and add more stock if the vegetables begin to dry out.

Roasting chicken joints. Use chicken joints, thighs, drumsticks or wings. Baste them with oil or melted butter and lay them on a rack in a roasting tin. To flavour them, either sprinkle them with chopped, fresh herbs; crumbled, dried herbs; or mix ground spices with the butter or oil.

Put them into the oven preheated to 400F / 200C / gas 6. Cook large joints for 35 - 45 minutes, small pieces for 30 minutes, or until they are golden brown and cooked through.

Grilling chicken joints. The joints can be grilled immediately after preparing or after

marinating.

To cook, brush the chicken joints with oil (preferably olive oil) and season them. You can also sprinkle them with chopped fresh or crumbled dried herbs or with spices such as paprika and cayenne pepper or a mixture of curry spices. For marinating, see page 13. The method of cooking is the same for both.

Preheat the grill under a high heat. Put the chicken joints on the hot rack, skin-side down first, and grill them until the side nearest the heat is golden brown. Turn them over and brown the other side. Continue to cook, turning the chicken pieces several times, until they are cooked through. Use the skewer test as for roasting. If the outside looks as though it will brown too much before the inside is done, lower the heat and lower the height of the chicken by taking away the grill rack.

Frying chicken joints. Use a large, heavy frying pan, big enough to take all the chicken pieces at one time. Use either 1 oz (25g) butter, or ½ oz (15g) butter plus 2 tablespoons olive or sunflower oil. Season the joints with pepper. Melt the butter, or butter and oil, in the frying pan on a medium heat. Put in the pieces, skin-side down first, and cook them until that side is brown. Turn them over and brown the other side. Lower the heat and continue cooking, turning several times, until the juices run clear when the thicker parts of meat are pierced with a skewer. Just before the joints are cooked, turn them skin-side up. Season them with pepper and a little salt and sprinkle over some chopped, fresh herbs, or crumbled, dried herbs.

Casseroling chicken joints. Melt 1 oz (25g)

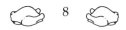

butter, or ½ oz (15g) butter plus 2 tablespoons olive or sunflower oil, in a wide based, flame-proof casserole on a medium heat. Put in the chicken joints, skin-side down first, and brown them on that side. Turn them and brown the other side. Remove them. Lower the heat. Put in one thinly sliced medium onion and soften it. Other vegetables such as celery, carrot or leek and a small amount of chopped bacon can also be added at this point. Pour in ½ pint (275ml) liquid. This can be chicken stock, white or red wine or cider, or a mixture of stock and alcohol. Bring it to the boil. Add a bouquet garni or chopped herbs and perhaps a flavouring such as tomato purée. Replace the chicken. Cover the casserole and put it into a preheated, 350F/180C/ gas 4 oven for 1 hour 15 minutes.

Cooking in a chicken brick. Chicken bricks are made from unglazed terracotta. When you first buy a brick, season it by brushing the inside with oil. Then place it into a preheated 425F/220C/gas 7 oven for 30 minutes. Let it cool. After this the brick should not be washed or immersed in water.

To cook a chicken in a brick, prepare it as for roasting. Heat the oven to 450F/230C/gas 8. Put the chicken into the brick and put on the lid. Put it into the oven for 1 hour 30 minutes.

To make gravy or sauce from the juices in the brick, pour them first into a saucepan and skim them.

Microwaving chicken. For a whole chicken use either a microwave tray with fitted lid or a tray that can be put into a roasting bag. Prepare the chicken as for roasting, rubbing spices into the skin, if wished, and spread it with a little sof-

tened butter or baste it with oil. Put it, breast side down, into the tray and either cover it with the lid or put it into the roasting bag. Microwave on high for 15 minutes. Turn the chicken breast-up and sprinkle it with chopped or dried herbs or lay herb sprigs over the breast and legs. Microwave on high for a further 15 minutes. Leave the chicken to stand for a further 15 minutes. Check to see that the juices run clear by pricking the thickest part of the meat with a fine skewer. If they do not, cook for a little longer, checking after each 5 minutes.

To cook chicken joints, use a microwave-proof dish with a lid. Put some chopped onion into the dish with either a little butter or oil, or some chopped bacon. Cover, and microwave on high for 4 minutes. Season the chicken joints and rub them with spices, if wished. Put them into the dish with their thicker parts towards the outside. Scatter them with chopped or dried herbs, if wished. Pour in ¼ pint (150ml) liquid such as stock wine, cider or sherry. Cover and microwave on high for 30 minutes. Leave to stand for 10 minutes before serving.

Pressure cooking chicken. Pressure cookers vary, so consult the manufacturer's instructions. The cooking time is calculated by weight so, if the chicken is stuffed, include the weight of the stuffing with that of the chicken. If you are cooking chicken portions, calculate the time by the weight of the largest portion. You do not increase the cooking time even if you are cooking eight rather than four portions. Season the chicken well for pressure cooking, and cover the portions with herb sprigs.

Barbecuing chicken. Whole chicken: cook on a spit roast over an open barbecue or on the rack in a kettle barbecue. For spit roasting, push the spit rod diagonally through the neck flap just below the breast bone and out just above the tail. Baste the chicken frequently as it cooks, with melted butter or oil. You can flavour the baste with spices if wished. One 3 - 3½ lb chicken should take about 1 hour 30 minutes, provided the heat is maintained at an even temperature.

For cooking in a kettle barbecue, put coals on either side of the barbecue with a drip-tray in the middle. Set the chicken above the drip tray and baste it as it cooks. One 3 - 3½ lb chicken will take 1 hour 30 minutes to 1 hour 45 minutes. Baste chicken joints and cook them for about 40 minutes over hot coals, turning them frequently.

CHICKEN STOCK

Chicken stock can be used to make gravies and sauces for your chicken dish, and any remaining makes excellent soup.

Use the chicken bones, plus the ends of the legs and wings. Use also the giblets if they have come with the chicken. Do not use the liver as this gives a bitter flavour.

Put the bones and giblets into a large saucepan. Add 1 carrot and a celery stick, roughly chopped, 1 onion, halved, and 1 tablespoon black peppercorns. Set the pan on a low heat and cook until the chicken pieces are lightly browned. Pour in cold water to the top of the pan. Add ½ teaspoon salt and a bouquet garni. Bring the water to the boil on a medium heat and skim if necessary. Cover and simmer for 1 hour. Strain the stock and cool it. Store it in the refrigerator in a covered container for up to one week.

SPICES TO FLAVOUR CHICKEN

For roasting, poaching or grilling, rub the skin with any one of these mixtures:

2 teaspoons paprika, quarter teaspoon cayenne pepper;

or 1 teaspoon each turmeric, ginger, cardamom;

or 1 teaspoon each cumin, coriander, curry powder;

or ½ teaspoon each allspice, cloves and cinnamon.

HERBS TO FLAVOUR CHICKEN

Parsley: Put large bunches inside chickens for roasting and into the water when poaching. Chop and add to stuffings and sauces. Use chopped parsley for garnishing hot dishes.

Thyme: Put about 4 sprigs inside a chicken for roasting or sprinkle in some dried thyme. Lay thyme sprigs over the breast and legs for roasting. Add 1 sprig to a bouquet garni for poaching. Chop and add to chicken casseroles and stuffings or sprinkle over grilled and fried chicken portions.

Marjoram: Use as thyme.

Chervil: Use as parsley.

Fennel: Excellent for using when the chicken is to be served cold. Put both inside and over the chicken for roasting, and inside and into the water for poaching. To flavour mayonnaise and salad dressings for chicken salads, use it chopped. Put a base of their stalks on the grill pan and cook chicken portions on top.

Lemon Balm: chop it and add it to stuffings.

Tarragon: Put sprigs inside and over a chicken for roasting. Chop and sprinkle over chicken as it is frying or grilling. Use chopped tarragon to flavour sauces and salad dressings.

Rosemary: Use very sparingly. It is best sprinkled over chicken as it is grilling or frying.

Sage: Although sage and onion stuffing is the most popular with chicken, it is not necessarily the best. Use sage very sparingly in stuffings, preferably with parsley and thyme or marjoram.

Dried mixed herbs: good for sprinkling inside a chicken for roasting.

MARINADES FOR CHICKEN

4 tablespoons each of olive oil and dry white wine, 1 small onion, chopped, 1 tablespoon each chopped thyme and marjoram;

4 tablespoons each of olive oil and dry white wine, 2 tablespoons chopped tarragon or fennel;

4 tablespoons each of olive oil and dry red wine, 1 small onion, chopped, 1 garlic clove, crushed, 1 tablespoon each of chopped thyme and marjoram;

4 tablespoons olive oil, juice ½ lemon, 2 teaspoons paprika, ¼ teaspoon cayenne pepper, 1 tablespoon tomato purée;

¼ pint (150ml) natural yoghurt, 1 teaspoon each of ground cumin, coriander, ginger and curry powder, 1 garlic clove, crushed, juice ½ lemon;

3 fl oz (90ml) dry cider, 4 tablespoons olive oil, 4 sage leaves, chopped, 1 teaspoon mustard

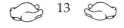

powder;

4 tablespoons each of olive oil and dry sherry, 2 tablespoons soy sauce, ½ oz (15g) fresh ginger root, peeled and grated, 6 spring onions, chopped, ½ teaspoon five-spice powder.

BASIC SAUCE FOR CHICKEN

l oz (25g) butter
l tablespoon flour
½ pint (275ml) chicken stock
2 tablespoons lemon juice
4 tablespoons double cream
herbs or spices to taste
seasoning to taste

Put the butter, flour and stock into a saucepan and stir on a medium heat until they come to the boil to make a thick sauce. Stir in the lemon juice. Take the pan from the heat and stir in the cream.

Add herbs to complement your dish after the sauce is made. Add up to 2 teaspoons spices with the flour. Add seasonings to taste.

BASIC STUFFING FOR CHICKEN

l oz (25g) butter
l small onion, finely chopped
3 oz (75g) wholemeal, granary or white breadcrumbs
up to 3 fl oz (90ml) liquid (stock, wine, cider, sherry)
herbs to taste
grated rind of lemon or orange to taste

Melt the butter in a small frying pan on a low

heat. Put in the onion and soften it. Mix in the breadcrumbs. Take the pan from the heat and stir in enough liquid to bind the mixture together. Add herbs plus orange or lemon rind if using.

Note: chickens are stuffed from the neck end.

GLOSSARY

Anchovy fillets: fillets of the anchovy fish that are salted and put into oil. They are about 4 inches (10 cm) long and are available tinned.

Bouquet garni: a bunch of herbs used to flavour casseroles, pot roasts, poached meats, soups and stews. Usually contains parsley, thyme, marjoram and a bay leaf. Sometimes pieces of leek and / or celery are tied in with the herbs. Bouquets garni made from dried herbs tied in muslin or in paper bags like tea bags are readily available.

Burghal wheat: also called bulgur or bulgar wheat. Made from whole wheat grains, soaked and then heated until they crack. Available from supermarkets and health shops.

Dijon Mustard: a mild French mustard.

Granary bread: the commercial name for bread made from flour containing the malted grains of wheat and barley.

Mace: mace is the outer coating of the nutmeg. Ground mace is a mild, yellow-coloured spice. If it is unavailable, use nutmeg.

Poppy seeds: small seeds from commercially produced poppies. They are available pale-coloured (known as white) or dark bluey-grey (known as black). Both taste the same but the black give a better appearance.

Sesame seeds: small, golden-brown, oval-shaped

seeds.

Tagliatelle: pasta made in ribbons.

Tahini: a thick paste made from crushed sesame seeds (rather like peanut butter). It is available from health shops.

TABLE OF OVEN TEMPERATURES

	Fahrenheit (F)	Celsius (C)	Gas mark
	150	70	
	175	80	
	200	100	
Very cool	225	110	¼
	250	120	½
	275	140	1
Cool	300	150	2
Warm	325	160	3
Moderate/ Medium	350	180	4
Fairly Hot	375	190	5
	400	200	6
Hot	425	220	7
	450	230	8
Very hot	475	240	9
	500	260	9

IMPERIAL/METRIC CONVERSIONS

Dry weight		**Liquid measure**	
ounces	grams	fluid ounces	millilitres
1	25	1	25
2	50	2	50
3	75	3	75-90
4 (¼ lb)	125	4	125
5	150	5 (¼ pint)	150
6	175	6	175
7	200	7	200
8 (½ lb)	225	8	225
9	250	9	250
10	275	10 (½ pint)	275
11	300	11	300
12 (¾ lb)	350	12	350
13	375	13	375
14	400	14	400
15	425	15 (¾ pint)	425
16 (1 lb)	450	16	450
17	475	17	475
18	500	18	500
2¼ lb	1000 (1 kilo)	20 (1 pint)	550
		1¾ pints	1000 (1 litre)

CHICKEN SALADS

Serves: 4 (each salad below)
Type of dish: two cold first courses
Suitable for main course: double ingredients
Preparation time: 20 minutes
Waiting time: nil
Cooking time: nil
Suitable for dinner parties: yes
Special equipment: none
Suitable for microwave cooking: chicken can be cooked initially
Suitable for pressure cooking: chicken can be cooked initially
Suitable for freezing: no
Calorie content: low
Carbohydrate content: medium
Fibre content: high
Protein content: medium
Fat content: low

 18

CHICKEN AND CARROT SALAD

4 oz (125g) cooked chicken
2 medium carrots
2 oz (50g) walnuts
1 oz (25g) raisins
1 tablespoon black poppy seeds
¼ pint (150ml) natural yoghurt
1 garlic clove, crushed with pinch salt
freshly ground black pepper
½ cucumber
4 walnut halves

Dice the chicken, grate the carrots and chop the walnuts. Put them into a bowl with the raisins and poppy seeds.

In another bowl, beat together the yoghurt, garlic and pepper. Fold the resulting dressing into the chicken mixture.

Thinly slice the cucumber. Arrange a ring of cucumber slices on each of four small serving plates and put a portion of salad in the centre. Garnish with the walnut halves.

☆ ☆ ☆

Chef's tips:
☆ This is a very suitable dish to make with leftover chicken. If you have insufficient meat, add extra chopped walnuts.
☆ Sunflower seeds may be used instead of walnuts. The garnish may then be a twist of lemon, or a sprig of parsley or watercress.
☆ The cucumber can be replaced by a 'nest' of

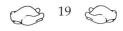

finely shredded salad leaves of different colours.

☆ Garlic bread makes a good accompaniment.

CHICKEN AND BROAD BEAN SALAD

4 oz (125g) cooked chicken
6 oz (175g) cooked broad beans (fresh, frozen or canned)
2 spring onions
4 tablespoons chopped parsley
3 tablespoons olive oil
1 tablespoon lemon juice
salt and freshly ground black pepper
1 small lettuce
4 small tomatoes

Dice the chicken. Chop the spring onions. In a bowl big enough to take all the ingredients, beat together the oil and lemon juice. Season. Fold in the chicken, beans and spring onions.

Arrange a bed of shredded lettuce on each of four small plates. Put a portion of the chicken salad on top. Garnish with wedges or slices of tomato.

☆　　☆　　☆

Chef's tips:
☆ As with the first recipe, this is an excellent way in which to serve up cold chicken. If you have insufficient meat, use extra broad beans or add some cooked haricot beans.
☆ Serve with hot brown rolls.

MARINATED CHICKEN ON STICKS

Serves: 4
Suitable for main course: double ingredients and
   use kebab skewers
Suitable for dinner party: yes
1st preparation time: 15 minutes
Waiting time: 2 hours
2nd preparation time: 20 minutes
Cooking time: 10 minutes
Special equipment: grill, 16 cocktail sticks
Suitable for microwave cooking: no
Suitable for pressure cooking: no
Suitable for freezing: no
Calorie content: medium
Carbohydrate content: low
Fibre content: low
Protein content: high
Fat content: medium

10 oz (275g) breast of chicken
1 tablespoon tahini (sesame paste)
3 fl oz (90ml) soy sauce
2 tablespoons sesame or sunflower or groundnut oil
3 spring onions, finely chopped
1 teaspoon freshly-grated ginger root or bottled ginger purée
1 garlic clove, crushed
1 small lettuce
1 red pepper
4 thin lemon slices

Cut the chicken into thirty-two small cubes.

Put the tahini into a bowl that is big enough to take all the chicken pieces and gradually stir in the soy sauce and the oil. Mix in the onions, ginger and garlic. Fold the chicken into the mixture, cover it and leave it for at least 2 hours at room temperature.

Just before cooking, arrange a bed of shredded lettuce on each of four small plates and cut the pepper into small, thin slivers. Thread two chicken pieces on to each cocktail stick. Heat the grill to a high heat and cook the chicken pieces for about 7 minutes, turning them several times, so they are cooked through and browned.

Lay four sticks of chicken on each plate and garnish them with the slivers of pepper. Make the lemon slices into twists and place one on each plate.

Chef's tips:

☆ The same marinade can be used for chicken thighs, drumsticks or portions which can then be either grilled or cooked in the oven and served as a main course.

☆ Tahini is the sesame seed equivalent of peanut butter. It can be bought from health food stores. If you have a choice between pale or darker coloured tahini, choose the pale coloured as it has a finer flavour. If tahini is not available, mix 1 tablespoon sesame oil into the marinade to give a nutty, sesame flavour.

☆ Serve with prawn crackers.

CHICKEN AND VEGETABLE SOUP

Serves: 6
Type of dish: Hot main course
Suitable for first course: in small quantities
1st preparation time: 5 minutes
2nd preparation time: 20 minutes
Cooking time: 1 hour 30 minutes
Waiting time: nil
3rd preparation time: 25 minutes
Suitable for dinner parties: no
Special equipment: food processor for chopping
    is an advantage
Suitable for microwave cooking: yes
Suitable for pressure cooking: yes
Suitable for freezing: yes
Calorie content: medium
Carbohydrate content: medium
Fibre content: high
Protein content: medium
Fat content: low

 25

One 3 - 3½ lb (1.25 - 1.6 kg) roasting chicken
4½ pints (2.575 litres) water
bouquet garni
salt and freshly-ground black pepper
2 oz (50g) long grain brown rice
2 medium potatoes
3 large carrots
4 celery sticks
1 large onion
2 leeks
8 oz (225g) swede or pumpkin
6 tablespoons chopped parsley

Put the chicken into a large saucepan (10 pint (5.75 litre) capacity if possible) and cover it with water. Add the bouquet garni and season well. Bring the water to the boil on a medium heat. Cover and simmer for 15 minutes. Put in the rice and cook for a further 45 minutes.

During this time, finely dice all the vegetables. A food processor will do this quickly and efficiently but it is not essential. Add the vegetables to the pan and continue cooking for 30 minutes more.

Take the pan from the heat and remove the chicken, holding it over the pan for a few seconds to let it drain well. Use two large forks if possible. Cut all the meat from the bones and dice it finely. Remove the bouquet garni from the soup and put in all the chicken meat. Reheat the soup gently.

Pour the soup into large, deep bowls. Scatter the parsley over the top.

☆   ☆   ☆

Chef's tips:
☆ Serve with hot rolls or with chunks of wholemeal bread.
☆ Use brown or white long grain rice.
☆ Pearl barley or rolled oats can be used instead of the rice.
☆ For extra flavour, add 3 - 5 fl oz (90 - 150ml) dry white wine to the soup just before the final reheating.

 27

☆ Grated Cheddar cheese can be scattered over the top of the soup.

☆ To freeze, cool the soup completely, put it into a rigid plastic container and cover it. Store for up to one month.

GRILLED SPICED CHICKEN

Serves: 4
Type of dish: Hot main course
Suitable for first course: Halve or quarter quantities and dice cooked chicken finely for a salad
Preparation time: 30 minutes
Waiting time: 6 hours
Cooking time: 25 minutes
Suitable for dinner parties: Yes.
Special equipment: Pestle and mortar; grill
Suitable for microwave cooking: yes
Suitable for pressure cooking: yes
Suitable for freezing: yes
Calorie content: medium
Carbohydrate content: low
Fibre content: low
Protein content: high
Fat content: medium

One 3 - 3½ lb (1.25 - 1.6 kg) roasting chicken
¼ pint (150ml) natural yoghurt
1 teaspoon whole coriander seeds
1 teaspoon whole cumin seeds
1 garlic clove, crushed with pinch salt
1 teaspoon ground ginger
juice ½ lemon
2 tablespoons chopped fresh coriander or parsley

Cut the chicken into four portions (page 5).

Put the yoghurt into an earthenware dish or plastic container that is big enough to take all the pieces of chicken. Using a pestle and mortar, crush the coriander and cumin seeds and mix them into the yoghurt together with the garlic, ginger and lemon juice. Turn the chicken pieces in the yoghurt, cover them with plastic film or with a lid and leave them at room temperature for 6 hours, turning them several times.

To cook, heat the grill to high. Lay the chicken pieces on the hot rack, skin-side down first, and grill them for about 20 minutes, or until they are golden brown on each side and completely cooked through, turning them several times. If the chicken pieces are browning too quickly, remove the grill rack before they are cooked through so they will not be seared by being too close to the heat.

Remove the grill rack and put the chicken into the bottom of the grill pan. If you have done this previously, simply cook the chicken in the grill pan until the juices run clear when the thicker parts of the meat are pierced with a skewer or fork. Spoon over any marinade that is still in the container and continue cooking on a slightly lower heat for a further 5 minutes so the marinade dries and browns.

Serve with the coriander or parsley scattered over the top.

☆　　☆　　☆

Chef's tips:

☆ Serve with spiced rice and a green salad. The chicken can either be placed on the rice or served separately.

☆ A mango or similar chutney makes a good accompaniment; or serve a raita consisting of diced cucumber mixed into natural yoghurt with a sprinkling of chopped, fresh mint.

☆ Ground cumin and coriander may be used if the whole seeds are not available.

☆ For a slightly hot flavour, add ¼ teaspoon cayenne pepper to the marinade.

☆ To freeze, cool the chicken completely and wrap it securely in plastic film. Keep it in the freezer for up to one month. Thaw in the refrigerator. Reheat by wrapping in foil and putting into a preheated 400F/200C/gas 6 oven for 15 minutes.

GRILLED CHICKEN WITH SPRING ONIONS

Serves: 4
Type of dish: Hot main course
Suitable for first course: no
Preparation time: 30 minutes
Waiting time: nil
Cooking time: 25 minutes
Suitable for dinner parties: yes
Special equipment: grill
Suitable for microwave cooking: yes
Suitable for pressure cooking: no
Suitable for freezing: yes
Calorie content: high
Carbohydrate content: low
Fibre content: low
Protein content: high
Fat content: high

33

One 3 - 3½ lb (1.25 - 1.6 kg) roasting chicken
2 tablespoons olive oil
freshly ground black pepper
4 tablespoons grated Parmesan cheese
4 tablespoons double cream
2 teaspoons Dijon or other French mustard
12 medium-sized spring onions

Cut the chicken into four joints (page 5). Brush the joints with the olive oil and grind over some pepper.

Put the Parmesan cheese into a bowl and, using a small wooden spoon, gradually mix in the cream and mustard. Finely chop the spring on-

ions and stir them into the cheese mixture so they are evenly distributed.

Preheat the grill to a high heat. Put the chicken portions on the hot rack, skin side down first, and grill them until they are cooked through and browned on each side, about 20 minutes. If the chicken pieces brown too quickly, either lower the position of the grill pan or remove the grill rack and cook the chicken in the base of the pan. (Further away from the heat, they will cook through but brown more slowly.) The chicken is done if the juices run clear when the thicker part of the meat is pierced with a skewer or fork.

Turn the chicken pieces skin-side up and spread the cheese and onion mixture over the skin, pressing it down in an even layer. Return the chicken pieces to the grill and cook until the surface of the topping is golden brown.

Chef's tips:
☆ To add colour garnish with grilled tomato halves, scattered with herbs.
☆ Serve either with tagliatelle tossed with butter and parsley; or with boiled potatoes, also tossed with butter and parsley; plus cooked green vegetables such as French beans, peas, or cauliflower.
☆ If spring onions are not available, use one small onion, very finely chopped.
☆ The Parmesan cheese may be replaced by 2 oz (50g) Gruyère or Emmenthal.
☆ To freeze, grill the chicken joints until they

are cooked through. Cool them completely. Make the topping and spread it over the chicken pieces. Wrap each chicken piece separately in plastic film. Store in the freezer for up to one month. Thaw in the refrigerator. Put the chicken pieces into an oven tin. Put them into a preheated 400F/200C/gas 6 oven for 15 minutes, or until the chicken is heated through and the topping is browned.

CHICKEN FRIED RICE WITH PINEAPPLE

Serves: 4
Type of dish: Hot main course
Suitable for first course: no
Preparation time: 30 minutes
Cooking time: 50 minutes
Waiting time: 30 minutes (overlaps cooking time)
Suitable for dinner parties: yes
Special equipment: wok or large, heavy frying pan
Suitable for microwave cooking: rice only
Suitable for pressure cooking: rice only
Suitable for freezing: yes
Calorie content: medium
Carbohydrate content: high
Fibre content: high
Protein content: medium
Fat content: medium

8 oz (225g) long grain brown rice
1 teaspoon salt
12 oz (350g) boneless chicken breasts
3 fl oz (90ml) soy sauce
2 eggs
1 large onion
2 green peppers
4 tablespoons sunflower or groundnut oil
1 garlic clove, finely chopped
4 slices pineapple, diced

Put the rice and salt into a saucepan with 1 pint (550ml) water. Bring them to the boil, cover and cook until the rice is tender and all the water has been absorbed, about 40 minutes.

Cut the chicken into small, thin slivers. Put 2 tablespoons of the soy sauce into a bowl and turn the chicken in it. Leave it for 30 minutes at room temperature.

Beat the eggs with the remaining soy sauce. Finely chop the onion. Core, seed and chop the peppers.

Heat the oil in a wok or a large, heavy frying pan on a high heat. Put in the pieces of chicken and stir-fry them for 1 minute. Put in the onion, peppers and garlic, lower the heat and continue to stir-fry for 5 minutes, or until the chicken pieces are cooked through.

Pour in the egg mixture and stir it until it just begins to scramble. Add the rice and continue to stir with a fork for 2 minutes, or until the rice is quite dry and has a light coating of egg. Mix

in the pineapple. Heat it through for 30 seconds and serve as soon as possible.

Chef's tips:
☆ Fresh or tinned pineapple may be used. As an alternative, use a carambola (star-fruit), cut into thin, star-shaped slices.
☆ Serve alone for a family meal, or, accompanied by other Chinese-style dishes as part of a Chinese dinner party.
☆ For a family meal, serve ungarnished. For a dinner party, garnish with spring onion brushes. To make these, cut spring onions into 3 inch (7.5 cm) lengths. Make several cuts down into

each end and soak the pieces in iced water for 30 minutes so that the cut ends curl outwards.

☆ To freeze, complete the dish without adding the pineapple. Cool it completely and pack it either into a rigid plastic container or into a strong polythene bag. Cover the container or seal the bag. Store for up to one month.

☆ Thaw in the refrigerator. Reheat by frying once more in a little hot oil in the wok or frying pan. Add the pineapple after reheating.

HOT SALAD OF CHICKEN, WHITE CABBAGE AND PEANUTS

Serves: 4

Type of dish: Hot main course

Suitable for first course: Use a small amount of finely chopped raw chicken, 6 oz (175g) cabbage and 1 oz (25g) peanuts

Preparation time: 40 minutes

Waiting time: nil

Cooking time: 35 minutes

Suitable for dinner parties: yes

Special equipment: large frying pan with lid

Suitable for microwave cooking: no

Suitable for pressure cooking: no

Suitable for freezing: no

Calorie content: high

Carbohydrate content: medium

Fibre content: medium

Protein content: high

Fat content: medium

One 3 - 3½ lb (1.25 - 1.6 kg) roasting chicken
1 tablespoon mustard powder
3 tablespoons olive or sunflower oil
1 tablespoon chopped rosemary, or 2 teaspoons dried rosemary, crumbled
1 medium onion
1 lb (450g) white cabbage
2 tablespoons white wine vinegar
2 oz (50g) shelled peanuts, unsalted

Cut the chicken into four joints (page 5). Rub the surface of the joints with half the mustard powder. Heat the oil in a large frying pan on a medium heat. Put in the chicken pieces, skin-side down, and cook them until the underside is golden brown, about 5 minutes. Turn them over and brown the other side. Turn them again. Turn the heat to low and scatter half the rosemary over the chicken. Cover the pan and cook the chicken pieces until they are tender and the juices run clear when the meat is pierced with a skewer, about 15 minutes.

While the chicken is cooking, thinly slice the onion and shred the cabbage. Mix together the remaining mustard and the vinegar. Take the chicken out of the pan and keep it warm.

Put in the onion, still over a low heat, and soften it. Turn the heat up to medium and stir in the cabbage, peanuts and remaining rosemary. Cook them, stirring, until the cabbage begins to wilt but is still crunchy, about 3 minutes. Pour in the vinegar and mustard mixture and bring

to the boil. Put back the chicken joints and keep the pan on a low heat for about 1 minute, for the flavours to blend.

To serve, set the chicken on top of the salad, either on individual plates or on one large serving plate.

☆   ☆   ☆

Chef's tips:
☆ Use one large serving dish for a dinner party and garnish the chicken with rosemary

sprigs, or with parsley sprigs if these are not available.

☆ Serve with jacket potatoes or new potatoes boiled in their skins and tossed with parsley and butter.

☆ If another vegetable is needed, choose something with a contrasting colour and texture, such as carrot.

CHICKEN WITH RED LENTILS

Serves: 4
Type of dish: Hot main course
Suitable for first course: no
Preparation time: 40 minutes
Waiting time: nil
Cooking time: 35 minutes
Suitable for dinner parties: yes
Special equipment: large frying pan with lid
Suitable for microwave cooking: no
Suitable for pressure cooking: yes
Suitable for freezing: yes
Calorie content: high
Carbohydrate content: medium
Fibre content: medium
Protein content: high
Fat content: medium

  45

One 3 lb (1.25 kg) roasting chicken
1 medium onion
1 oz (25g) butter
8 oz (225g) split red lentils
1 teaspoon paprika
pinch cayenne pepper, or more to taste
¾ pint (425ml) tomato and vegetable juice
1½ pints (850ml) chicken stock
1 teaspoon dried mixed herbs

Cut the chicken into four joints and then each joint into two pieces (page 5). Finely chop the onion.

Melt the butter in a flameproof casserole on a medium heat. Put in the chicken pieces, skin-side down first, and brown them on both sides. Remove them.

Lower the heat, put in the onion and soften it. Stir in the lentils, paprika and cayenne pepper and stir them on the heat for about one minute. Pour in the tomato and vegetable juice and the stock and bring them to the boil. Add the mixed herbs and replace the chicken. Cover and simmer gently for 1 hour 15 minutes so the chicken is tender and the lentils have cooked to a soft purée.

Chef's tips:
☆ Garnish, if wished, with chopped parsley.
☆ Serve with rice or with jacket potatoes and a green vegetable or salad.
☆ Plain tomato juice can be used if tomato and vegetable juice is not available.
☆ To freeze, cool completely, pack into a rigid plastic container and cover. Store for up to one month. Thaw gently in the refrigerator and reheat by putting into a casserole and into a preheated 350F/180C/gas 4 oven for 20 - 30 minutes.

CHICKEN WITH CELERY AND CHEDDAR CHEESE STUFFING

Serves: 4
Type of dish: Hot main course
Suitable for first course: no
1st preparation time: 30 minutes
Waiting time: nil
Cooking time: 1 hour 30 minutes
2nd preparation time: 15 minutes
Suitable for dinner parties: yes
Special equipment: frying pan, roasting tin, oven
Suitable for microwave cooking: yes
Suitable for pressure cooking: yes
Suitable for freezing: no
Calorie content: high
Carbohydrate content: medium
Fibre content: medium
Protein content: high
Fat content: high

 48

One 3 - 3½ lb (1.25 - 1.6 kg) roasting chicken
4 small celery sticks, from the inside of the head
1 small onion
2 oz (50g) Cheddar cheese
1 oz (25g) butter
2 oz (50g) wholemeal breadcrumbs
2 tablespoons chopped parsley
1 tablespoon chopped thyme, or 1 teaspoon dried
2 tablespoons dry white wine
½ pint (275ml) chicken stock

Heat the oven to 400F/200C/gas 6. Finely chop the celery and onion and finely dice the cheese.

Melt the butter in a frying pan on a low heat. Mix in the celery and onion and soften them. Take the pan from the heat and mix in the breadcrumbs and herbs and finally the cheese, taking care not to mash it or break it up. Mix in the wine.

Use the mixture to stuff the chicken. Truss the chicken (page 4) and put it into a roasting tin. Cover it completely with foil and put it into the oven for 1 hour. Remove the foil and continue cooking for a further 30 minutes or until the skin is crisp and golden brown.

Remove the chicken to a carving plate. Pour any excess fat from the tin and set the tin back on top of the stove on a medium heat. Pour in the stock and stir well to incorporate any residue that is in the bottom of the pan. Simmer the resulting gravy gently while you carve the chicken into four portions.

Arrange the chicken portions on a dish with

 49

the stuffing and serve the gravy separately.

Chef's tips:
☆ Garnish with watercress sprigs.
☆ Serve with roast potatoes or with potato slices roasted until they are crisp in a mixture of oil and butter; plus a selection of lightly cooked vegetables of contrasting colours and textures.
☆ Dice leftover roast chicken and mix it with diced celery and a mayonnaise dressing, to make a chicken salad.

PARSLEY CHICKEN

Serves: 4
Type of dish: Hot main course
Suitable for first course: no
Preparation time: 30 minutes
Waiting time: nil
Cooking time: 1 hour 30 minutes
Suitable for dinner parties: yes
Special equipment: frying pan, roasting tin, oven
Suitable for microwave cooking: yes
Suitable for pressure cooking: yes
Suitable for freezing: no
Calorie content: high
Carbohydrate content: low
Fibre content: low
Protein content: high
Fat content: medium

One 3 - 3½ lb (1.25 - 1.6 kg) roasting chicken
Stuffing:
1 small onion
½ oz (15g) butter
3 oz (75g) granary or wholemeal breadcrumbs
3 tablespoons chopped parsley
grated rind and juice ½ lemon
Roasting:
2 oz (50g) butter, softened
3 tablespoons chopped parsley
Sauce:
1 tablespoon flour
¾ pint (425ml) chicken stock
3 tablespoons chopped parsley
juice ½ lemon

Heat the oven to 400F/200C/gas 6.

For the *stuffing,* finely chop the onion. Melt the butter in a frying pan on a low heat. Put in the onion and soften it. Take the pan from the heat and mix in the breadcrumbs, parsley and lemon juice. Use the mixture to stuff the chicken.

Truss the chicken (page 4) and put it into a roasting tin. Work the softened butter and the parsley together and spread them over the surface of the chicken. Cover the chicken completely with foil and put it into the oven for 1 hour. Remove the foil and continue to cook the chicken for about 30 minutes until the skin is golden brown and crisp. Put the chicken on a carving plate and keep it warm.

Pour off all but 2 tablespoons of fat from the roasting tin and set the tin on top of the stove on a medium heat. Stir in the flour and stock. Bring them to the boil and stir in the parsley and lemon juice.

Carve the chicken into four pieces and arrange them on a warm serving dish with the stuffing. Serve the sauce separately.

Chef's tips:

☆ Garnish with parsley sprigs and twists of lemon, if wished.

☆ Serve with roast potatoes, new potatoes or with potato slices roasted until crisp in a mixture of oil and butter; plus a selection of lightly cooked vegetables or a green salad.

☆ Dice leftover chicken and make into a salad with a parsley and yoghurt dressing.

CHICKEN, COURGETTE AND TOMATO SALAD

Serves: 4
Type of dish: cold main course
Suitable for first course: in small quantities
1st preparation time: 10 minutes
1st cooking time: 1 hour 15 minutes
2nd preparation time: 30 minutes
2nd cooking time: 15 minutes
Waiting time: 2 - 3 hours (for cooling)
3rd preparation time: 15 minutes
Suitable for dinner parties: yes and buffets
Special equipment: saucepan
Suitable for microwave cooking: the chicken can be cooked initially
Suitable for pressure cooking: yes, initially
Suitable for freezing: no
Calorie content: medium
Carbohydrate content: low
Fibre content: medium
Protein content: high
Fat content: medium

One 3 - 3½ lb (1.25 - 1.6kg) chicken
1 oz (25g) butter, softened
2 teaspoons paprika
½ teaspoon cayenne pepper
bouquet garni
1 lb (450g) small courgettes
1 large onion
4 tablespoons olive oil
1 garlic clove, finely chopped
1 teaspoon paprika
2 tablespoons chopped chervil or parsley
2 tablespoons dry white wine, or 1 tablespoon white wine vinegar
12 oz (350g) tomatoes

Heat the oven to 400F/200C/gas 6. Spread the butter over the breast of the chicken. Sprinkle the whole chicken with the paprika and cayenne pepper. Put the bouquet garni inside. Truss the chicken, cover it with foil and put it into the oven for 1 hour. Remove the foil and continue to cook for 30 minutes. Take the chicken from the oven, cool it slightly and dice it.

Thinly slice the courgettes and onion.

Heat the oil in a saucepan on a low heat. Put in the onion and garlic, cover and cook for 5 minutes. Stir in the courgettes and paprika. Cover and cook for 10 minutes more. Mix in the chicken. Take the pan off the heat and mix in the chervil or parsley and the wine or vinegar. Turn the mixture into a bowl and let cool completely.

Cut the tomatoes first in half lengthways and then into slices crossways. Mix them into the salad just before serving.

☆   ☆   ☆

Chef's tips:
☆ Garnish with chervil or parsley sprigs; or with mustard and cress. Alternately, serve surrounded by very finely shredded salad leaves.
☆ Serve with a potato or rice salad.
☆ The salad can also be made with a bought roast chicken.
☆ The salad can be made with leftover roast chicken from another meal. If there is insufficient meat add some cooked haricot or flageolet beans.

 57

COATED CHICKEN DRUMSTICKS

Serves: 4 (each recipe)
Type of dish: Hot or cold main course or picnic
Suitable for first course: no
Preparation time: 30 minutes
Waiting time: nil
Cooking time: 30 minutes
Suitable for dinner parties: buffet parties
Special equipment: oven tin with wire rack
Suitable for microwave cooking: no
Suitable for pressure cooking: no
Suitable for freezing: yes
Calorie content: high
Carbohydrate content: low
Fibre content: low
Protein content: high
Fat content: medium

12 chicken drumsticks
Oat coating:
5 oz (150g) porridge oats
½ oz (15g) Parmesan cheese
2 teaspoons dried mixed herbs
3 tablespoons olive or sunflower oil
2 eggs, beaten
2 oz (50g) wholemeal flour
Sesame coating:
1 tablespoon tahini (sesame paste)
4 tablespoons olive or sunflower oil
1 tablespoon tomato purée
1 tablespoon white wine vinegar
pinch chili powder
2 oz (50 g) sesame seeds

For either coating, heat the oven to 400F / 200C / gas 6.

To make the *oat coating*, mix together the oats, Parmesan cheese, herbs and oil. Dip the chicken drumsticks in the beaten egg, roll them in the flour and dip them again into the egg. Roll them in the oat mixture to coat them completely.

For the *sesame coated drumsticks*, beat together the tahini, oil, tomato purée, vinegar and chili powder. Coat the chicken pieces in the mixture and roll them in the sesame seeds.

Regardless of coating, put the drumsticks on a rack in an oven tin and cook them for 35 minutes or until they are golden brown and cooked through. If serving them cold, cool them on the rack.

Chef's tips:

☆ Serve garnished with watercress sprigs and wedges of tomato.

☆ As a hot meal, serve with sauté potatoes or potatoes that have been sliced and roasted in a mixture of oil and butter; plus a salad.

☆ As a cold meal, serve with a selection of salads including one based on rice or potatoes.

☆ For a mixed buffet meal or for a picnic for more than four people, make both kinds of drumsticks.

☆ To freeze, cool the drumsticks completely. Freeze them separately, on a tray, then pack them into boxes. Cook from frozen. Put the drumsticks on a wire rack in an oven tin and put them into the oven for 20 minutes or until they are completely heated through.

POACHED SPICED CHICKEN WITH LEEKS

Serves: 4
Type of dish: Hot main course
Suitable for first course: no
1st preparation time: 10 minutes
Waiting time: nil
Cooking time: 1 hour
2nd preparation time: 30 minutes
Suitable for dinner parties: yes
Special equipment: large saucepan or casserole;
     perforated spoon
Suitable for microwave cooking: yes
Suitable for pressure cooking: yes
Suitable for freezing: yes
Calorie content: high
Carbohydrate content: low
Fibre content: low
Protein content: high
Fat content: medium

One 3 - 3½ lb (1.25 - 1.6kg) roasting chicken
½ lemon, sliced
1 teaspoon ground cumin
1 teaspoon ground coriander
1 lb (450g) leeks
sauce:
1 oz (25g) butter
1 teaspoon ground cumin
1 teaspoon ground coriander
1 tablespoon flour
½ pint (275ml) poaching liquid
juice ½ lemon
2 tablespoons chopped parsley

Put the sliced lemon inside the chicken and rub the spices into the skin. Cut the leeks into 1½ inch (4 cm) lengths.

Put the chicken into a large saucepan or flame-proof casserole and surround it with the leeks. Pour in water to just cover the legs of the chicken. Set the pan on a medium heat and bring the water to the boil. Cover and simmer for 50 minutes, or until the chicken is tender.

Lift out the chicken and let it cool slightly. Lift out the leeks with a perforated spoon. Reserve them.

For the *sauce,* strain off ½ pint (275ml) of the poaching liquid. Melt the butter in a saucepan on a low heat and cook the spices gently in it for 2 minutes. Stir in the flour and the stock. Bring the sauce to the boil, stirring. Add the lemon juice and parsley and simmer for 2 minutes.

Cut the chicken into 1 inch (2.5 cm) dice. Fold

the chicken and leeks into the sauce. Reheat gently, without letting the chicken overcook.

☆   ☆   ☆

Chef's tips:
☆ Serve either from a serving dish or on individual plates. Garnish, if wished, with one leek, cut into small, thin slivers, blanched in boiling water for 2 minutes and drained. Parsley sprigs or chopped parsley can be used instead.

☆ Serve with rice that has been cooked in some of the poaching liquid; or with boiled potatoes tossed with butter and herbs; plus either a selection of lightly cooked vegetables, such as courgettes and carrots, or a green salad that includes slices of orange.

☆ The completed dish can be frozen in the sauce. Cool it completely and pack it into a rigid plastic container. Cover it and store it for up to one month. Thaw in the refrigerator and reheat gently in a saucepan.

MIDDLE EASTERN CHICKEN SALAD

Serves: 4
Type of dish: Cold main course
Suitable for first course: no
1st preparation time: 15 minutes
Cooking time: 1 hour
Waiting time: 2 hours (for cooling)
2nd preparation time: 40 minutes
Suitable for dinner parties: yes, and buffet parties
Special equipment: large saucepan or casserole
Suitable for microwave cooking: yes
Suitable for pressure cooking: yes
Suitable for freezing: no
Calorie content: high
Carbohydrate content: high
Fibre content: high
Protein content: high
Fat content: medium

One 3 - 3½ lb (1.25 - 1.6 kg) roasting chicken
½ lemon, thinly sliced
1 teaspoon ground cinnamon
1 teaspoon ground ginger
For boiling:
1 small onion, halved
1 medium carrot, roughly chopped
1 medium celery stick, roughly chopped
bouquet garni
1 teaspoon black peppercorns
Salad:
¼ pint (150ml) natural yoghurt
½ teaspoon ground cinnamon
½ teaspoon ground ginger
3 oz (75g) stoned dates
8 oz (225g) burghul wheat
4 tablespoons olive oil
juice ½ lemon
1 garlic clove, crushed with pinch salt
3 tablespoons chopped parsley
freshly ground black pepper
½ lemon, thinly sliced

Truss the chicken (page 4), putting the lemon inside. Mix together the cinnamon and ginger and rub them into the chicken skin. Put the chicken into a saucepan with the boiling ingredients and pour in water to just above the top of the legs. Bring to the boil, cover and simmer for 50 minutes, or until the chicken is tender. Lift out the chicken and cool it completely.

For the *salad*, soak the burghul wheat in cold

 66

water for 30 minutes. Cut all the chicken meat from the bones, dice it and put it into a bowl. Mix the yoghurt with the spices and fold it into the chicken. Add the dates.

Drain the wheat and squeeze it dry. In a large bowl, beat together the oil, lemon juice and garlic. Fold in the wheat.

Put a ring of wheat round the edge of a large, flat serving dish. Put the chicken salad in the centre and garnish with the lemon slices.

Chef's tips:

☆ Small parsley sprigs can be used to give additional colour.

☆ Serve with a green salad.

☆ Burghul wheat is also called bulgar or bulgur wheat. It can be bought from health food stores.

HERBY CHICKEN WITH NUT TOPPING

Serves: 4
Type of dish: Hot main course
Suitable for first course: no
1st preparation time: 30 minutes
Waiting time: 12 hours
2nd preparation time: 20 minutes
Cooking time: 45 minutes
Suitable for dinner parties: yes
Special equipment: oven-to-table dish
Suitable for microwave cooking: yes
Suitable for pressure cooking: no
Suitable for freezing: yes
Calorie content: high
Carbohydrate content: low
Fibre content: low
Protein content: high
Fat content: high

One 3 - 3½ lb (1.25 - 1.6 kg) roasting chicken
4 tablespoons olive oil
juice 1 lemon
3 tablespoons chopped parsley
1 tablespoon chopped thyme (or 1 teaspoon dried)
1 tablespoon chopped marjoram (or 1 teaspoon dried)
1 teaspoon chopped sage (or ½ teaspoon dried)
1 medium onion, finely chopped
1½ oz (40g) shelled walnuts
1½ oz (40g) shelled hazelnuts

Cut the chicken into 8 serving pieces (page 5). In a dish or plastic container, big enough to take all the chicken pieces, mix together the oil, lem-

on juice, herbs and onion. Turn the chicken in the mixture and leave it, covered, for 12 hours at room temperature.

To cook, heat the oven to 400F/200C/gas 6. Lift out the chicken pieces, brushing any pieces of onion from them, and reserve the marinade. Put the chicken pieces, attractively arranged and skin-side up, into a shallow, oven-to-table dish. Put it into the oven for 30 minutes.

While the chicken is cooking, grind the nuts in a blender, food processor or coffee grinder, or very finely chop them. Mix them to a paste with the reserved marinade. Spread the paste evenly over the chicken pieces and return the chicken to the oven for a further 45 minutes.

Serve straight from the dish.

☆   ☆   ☆

Chef's tips:
☆ Garnish with parsley sprigs before serving, if wished.
☆ Serve with boiled new potatoes or with sautéed potatoes; plus either a selection of green vegetables or a green salad.
☆ The chicken may be cooled completely in the dish and served as a cold meal.
☆ Natural yoghurt may be used in place of the olive oil.
☆ Brazil nuts can be used in place of either the walnuts or the hazelnuts.
☆ 1 oz (25g) finely chopped dried apricots may be mixed into the nuts.
☆ If you have used a container that is both ovenproof and freezerproof, the chicken can be

frozen as it is. Cool it completely and cover it. Store for up to one month. The chicken along with the cooking juices can also be lifted carefully into a rigid plastic container and covered. To reheat, thaw in the refrigerator, bring to room temperature and put into a preheated 400F/200C/gas 6 oven for 15 minutes, having first transferred the chicken to a suitable container if it has been stored in plastic.

CHICKEN WITH AVOCADO

Serves: 4
Type of dish: hot main course
Suitable for first course: no
Preparation time: 45 minutes
Waiting time: nil
Cooking time: 45 minutes
Suitable for dinner parties: yes
Special equipment: oven-to-table dish
Suitable for microwave cooking: yes
Suitable for pressure cooking: no
Suitable for freezing: no
Calorie content: high
Carbohydrate content: low
Fibre content: low
Protein content: high
Fat content: high

 73

One 3 lb (1.25 kg) roasting chicken
4 tablespoons olive or sunflower oil
2 medium onions, thinly sliced
2 teaspoons paprika
¼ teaspoon cayenne pepper
2 ripe avocados
4 tablespoons natural yoghurt
1 garlic clove, crushed with pinch salt

Heat the oven to 400F/200C/gas 6. Cut the chicken into 8 serving pieces (page 5). Brush them with 1 tablespoon of the oil and grill them under a high grill until they are just beginning to brown on both sides.

Heat the remaining oil in a frying pan on a low heat. Put in the onions and soften them. Take the pan from the heat and mix in half the paprika and cayenne pepper. Choose an oven-to-table dish which is fairly shallow and which will take all the chicken pieces in one layer. Put the onions into the bottom of the dish and put the chicken pieces on top, skin-side up.

Peel the avocados and mash them to a purée. Mix in the remaining paprika and cayenne pepper and the yoghurt. Spoon the avocado evenly over the chicken. Cover the dish with foil and put it into the oven for 45 minutes. Serve the chicken straight from the dish.

Chef's tips:
☆ Garnish with parsley sprigs, tomato slices

or wedges of lemon.

☆ Serve with rice that has been cooked with paprika, cayenne pepper and tomato purée; plus either a green salad, or a cooked dish of peppers and courgettes or aubergines.

☆ To mash the avocados, peel them and remove the stones. Put them into a bowl and use a potato masher to reduce them to a smooth purée. Then gradually work in the other ingredients.

CHICKEN WITH RED AND GREEN PEPPERS

Serves: 4
Type of dish: hot main course
Suitable for first course: no
Preparation time: 30 minutes
Waiting time: nil
Cooking time: 1 hour 30 minutes
Suitable for dinner parties: yes
Special equipment: flameproof casserole
Suitable for microwave cooking: yes
Suitable for pressure cooking: yes
Suitable for freezing: yes
Calorie content: medium
Carbohydrate content: low
Fibre content: low
Protein content: high
Fat content: medium

One 3 - 3½ lb (1.25 - 1.6 kg) roasting chicken
2 large red peppers
1 large green pepper
8 oz (225g) button mushrooms
1 large onion
4 tablespoons olive or sunflower oil
¼ pint (150 ml) chicken stock
¼ pint (150 ml) dry sherry (for a family meal, use all stock)
1 tablespoon chopped thyme (or 1 teaspoon dried)

Heat the oven to 350F/180C/gas 4. Cut the chicken into four serving pieces (page 5). Core the peppers and remove the pith and seeds. Cut the peppers into strips about 1 inch by ¼ inch (2.5 cm by 6 mm). Thinly slice the mushrooms. Quarter and thinly slice the onion.

Heat the oil in a large, flameproof casserole on a medium heat. Put in the chicken pieces, skin-side down first and brown them on both sides. This will take about 15 minutes. Remove the chicken pieces. Put in the onion and garlic and soften them. Mix in the peppers and mushrooms. Pour in the stock and sherry or the stock alone and bring the liquid to the boil. Sprinkle in the thyme and return the chicken joints to the casserole, skin-side up and overlapping as little as possible.

Cover the casserole and put it into the oven for 1 hour 30 minutes.

☆　　☆　　☆

Chef's tips:

☆ Transfer to one large dish or to individual plates for serving.

☆ A scattering of chopped parsley can be used for garnish.

☆ Serve with lightly cooked tagliatelle tossed with butter and Parmesan cheese; plus either a salad or cooked courgettes or mange tout peas.

☆ This dish can be cooked in advance and re-heated gently at the same oven temperature for 20 minutes.

☆ To freeze: cool completely, pack into a rigid plastic container and cover. Store for up to one month. Thaw in the refrigerator and reheat in ered casserole in the oven for 20 minutes.

CHICKEN AND BACON
PUDDING

Serves: 4
Type of dish: hot main course
Suitable for first course: no
Preparation time: 40 minutes
Waiting time: nil
Cooking time: 1 hour 30 minutes
Suitable for dinner parties: no
Special equipment: pudding basin
Suitable for microwave cooking: yes
Suitable for pressure cooking: yes
Suitable for freezing: yes
Calorie content: high
Carbohydrate content: medium
Fibre content: medium
Protein content: high
Fat content: high

6 oz (175g) chicken breast
4 oz (125g) green back bacon
4 oz (125g) mushrooms
1 medium onion
grated rind 1 lemon
¼ teaspoon ground mace
4 tablespoons chopped parsley
freshly ground black pepper
8 oz (225g) wholemeal flour
1 teaspoon bicarbonate of soda
¼ teaspoon salt
2 oz (50g) vegetable suet
2 eggs, beaten
4 tablespoons cold water
Sauce:
½ pint (275 ml) chicken stock
1 oz (25 g) butter
1 tablespoon wholemeal flour
1 tablespoon Worcester sauce
1 tablespoon mushroom ketchup
3 tablespoons chopped parsley

Finely dice the chicken and bacon and chop the mushrooms and onion. Mix all these in a bowl and mix in the lemon, mace, parsley and pepper.

Put the flour into a bowl with the bicarbonate of soda, salt and suet. Mix it to a dough with the eggs and as much cold water as is necessary. Set aside about one quarter of the dough to make the top of the pudding. Use the rest to line a 2 pint (1.15 litre) pudding basin. Put in the chick-

en mixture. Cover it with the remaining dough and seal the edges. Cover the basin with a layer of buttered greaseproof paper and one of foil. Tie them down with string, making a handle.

Bring a large pan of water to the boil. Lower in the pudding. Cover the pan and simmer the pudding for 1 hour 30 minutes, topping up the water as and when necessary.

When it is ready, lift the pudding out of the saucepan and serve it straight from the basin.

To make the *sauce,* put all the ingredients except the parsley into a saucepan. Set them on a medium heat and stir with a wooden spoon until they come to the boil. Take the pan from the heat and stir in the parsley.

Chef's tips:
☆ Serve with plainly boiled potatoes, tossed with butter and parsley; plus a green vegetable such as cabbage or broccoli and a contrasting root vegetable: carrot or swede, depending on the season. Serve the sauce separately.
☆ The bacon may be replaced with lean cooked ham.
☆ To freeze, cool the pudding completely in the basin. Replace the greaseproof and foil coverings and put the basin into a polythene bag. Store for up to one month. Thaw in the refrigerator and then bring to room temperature. To reheat, lower the pudding into boiling water and cook it for 45 minutes.

RAISED CHICKEN AND LEEK PIE

Serves: 6
Type of dish: cold main course or buffet
Suitable for first course: no
Preparation time: 1 hour 15 minutes
Cooking time: 2 hours
Waiting time: 6 hours (for cooling)
Suitable for dinner parties: yes
Special equipment: 2 lb (900g) raised pie mould
   or loaf tin
Suitable for microwave cooking: no
Suitable for pressure cooking: no
Suitable for freezing: yes
Calorie content: high
Carbohydrate content: medium
Fibre content: low
Protein content: high
Fat content: medium

One 3 lb (1.25 kg) roasting chicken
4 oz (125g) smoked streaky bacon
12 oz (350g) leeks
3 tablespoons chopped parsley
6 sage leaves, chopped (or 1½ teaspoons dried sage)
freshly ground black pepper
salt
Pastry:
1 lb (450g) plain flour
½ teaspoon salt
freshly ground black pepper
4 tablespoons milk
3 tablespoons water
5 oz (150g) lard
1 egg, beaten (for glaze)

Heat the oven to 325F/160C/gas 3.

Joint the chicken. Take all the meat from the bones and dice it. Dice the bacon. Cut each leek in half lengthways and slice it thinly. In a bowl, mix together the chicken, bacon, leeks, parsley sage and seasonings.

To make the *pastry*, put the flour into a bowl with the salt and pepper and make a well in the centre. Put the lard, milk and water into a saucepan and set them on a low heat for the lard to melt. Pour the mixture into the flour and quickly mix everything into a workable dough.

Set aside one third of the dough for the top of the pie. Use the rest to line a 2 lb (900g) raised pie mould or loaf tin. Press in the chicken mixture and cover it with the reserved pastry. Seal

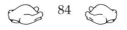

the edges, making sure that they come inside the rim of the tin or mould. Brush the top of the pie with beaten egg and decorate the top with any trimmings. Brush with egg again.

Bake the pie for 2 hours. Take it out of the oven and let it stand for 10 minutes. Remove the mould. To turn it out of the loaf tin, gently loosen the sides of the pie using a rounded knife. Turn the pie out of the tin onto a rack and immediately turn it the right way up again.

Cool the pie on the rack for at least 6 hours before serving.

Chef's tips:
☆ Serve with a selection of salads as a cold meal.
☆ To freeze, cool the pie completely. Seal it in a polythene bag and store it in the freezer where it is not going to get crushed. Thaw in the refrigerator and then bring it up to room temperature.

Chicken and Onion Quiche

CHICKEN AND ONION QUICHE

Serves: 4

Type of dish: hot or cold main course or buffet dish

Suitable for first course: yes, cut into small slices

Preparation time: 40 minutes

Waiting time: nil

Cooking time: 25 minutes

Suitable for dinner parties: yes

Special equipment: 8 inch (20 cm) diameter tart tin

Suitable for microwave cooking: yes

Suitable for pressure cooking: no

Suitable for freezing: yes

Calorie content: high

Carbohydrate content: medium

Fibre content: medium

Protein content: high

Fat content: high

Pastry:		
3 oz (75g) wholemeal flour		
3 oz (75g) plain flour		
pinch salt		
3 oz (75g) butter		
water to mix		
Filling:		
8 oz (225g) cold cooked chicken		
12 oz (350g) onions		
½ oz (15g) butter		
2 tablespoons olive oil		
3 eggs		
4 tablespoons milk		
2 tablespoons chopped parsley		
1 tablespoon chopped thyme (or 1 teaspoon dried)		
6 anchovy fillets		
8 black olives		

Heat the oven to 400F/200C/gas 6.

To make the *pastry*, put the flours into a bowl with the salt. Rub in the butter and mix in enough water to make a workable dough. Leave the dough in a cool place for 15 minutes.

For the *filling* dice the chicken. Thinly slice the onions and soften them in the butter and oil on a low heat. Cool them. In a large bowl, beat together the eggs and milk. Fold in the chicken, onions, parsley and thyme.

Line an 8 inch (20 cm) diameter tart tin with the pastry. Put in the chicken filling. Cut the anchovies in half lengthways and arrange them in